How to Setup & Repair a Complete Skateboard
by Tim Swike

Please Read This FIRST

Terms of Use

This Electronic book is Copyright © 2007. All rights reserved. No part of this book may be reproduced, stored in a retrieval system, or transmitted by any means; electronic, mechanical, photocopying, recording or otherwise, without written permission from the copyright holder(s).

WARNING!

Skateboarding can be dangerous and can cause injuries. <u>All</u> readers must accept sole responsibility for their use of this guide and the material in it including any personal injury, property damage or other consequences.

USE AT YOUR OWN RISK.

Disclaimer

The advice contained in this material might not be suitable for everyone. The author provided the information only as a broad overview by a lay person about an important subject. The author used information from sources believed to be reliable and from his own personal experience, but he neither implies nor intends any guarantee of accuracy. The results you obtain will depend largely on your own efforts, climatic and other factors beyond the knowledge and control of the author, publisher and distributors. No particular result or outcome is promised or guaranteed in any way.

New theories and practices are constantly being developed in this area.

The author, publisher and distributors never give legal, accounting, medical or any other type of professional advice. The reader must always seek those services from competent professionals that can apply the latest technical information and review their own particular circumstances.

The author, publisher and distributors particularly disclaim any liability, loss, or risk taken by individuals who directly or indirectly act on the information contained herein. All readers must accept full responsibility for their use of this material.

All pictures used in this book are for illustrative purposes only.

Contents

Please Read This FIRST 2
    Terms of Use 2
    WARNING! 2
    Disclaimer 2

Contents 4

Introduction 6
    Installing the Griptape 7

Installing the Hardware 16

Installing the Riser Pads 18

Installing the Trucks 19
    Be Careful 20

Installing the Wheels and Bearings 21
    Install Bearing Spacers 22

Using a Bearing Press 27

Adjusting the Trucks 28
    Break In Your Skateboard. 30

Some Common Skateboard Repairs 31
    Changing the Griptape 31
    Cleaning the Bearings 32
    Ultra-cleaning the Bearings 33

Choosing and Using Lubricants 38

Changing the Kingpin Bushings and Pivot Bushing 39
    Replacing the Small Pivot Bushing 40

Changing the Kingpin 42
    Install the New Kingpin. 44
        Replacing a Kingpin Without a Vice 45

Great Answers to Common Questions. 47
    What types of varnishes do skateboard decks have? 47
        Choosing Among Varnish Products 48
        The Varnish We Chose 49
        Finishing 50
    How can graphics and finishes affect a skateboard's performance? 51
        Heat Transfers 51

- Silk-Screening 51
- Ultra Violet Painting 52
- Clear Coating 52
- SST Coating 52
- Shrink Wrap 52
- Summary 53

When considering skateboard deck concaves, how steep is too steep? 54

Can you tell me something I don't already know about skateboard decks? 56
- Why is Maple the Best Choice? 56
- What is the Best Maple Skateboard deck on the market? 56
- What Makes a Board Pop Good? 56
- How Does Moisture Content Affect Strength? 57
- Why Do Boards Chip, Delaminate, and Snap in Half? 57
- How is a Skateboard Made? 58

Will the skateboarding industry quit using wood and start using more composites? 59

Why do some decks delaminate? 60
- Drying Times 60
- Pressing the Wood 60
- Glue Use 61

When do I need to use riser pads? 62

Which Bearings are Better; ABEC 3, ABEC 5 or ABEC 7? 63

What Kind of Wheels are Best for Skateboarding? 65

How Do I Break My Bearings in? 68

What Kind of Wheel Lubricant Should I Buy for my Bearings? 69

What are the Best Bearings to Skate with? 70

How do Trucks Work? 71

What are stress cracks? 72

What do I do if My Deck Chips or Cracks? 73

Summary 76

Introduction

Thanks for purchasing this skateboard guide. I have good news. In a couple of minutes you will be an expert at basic skateboard setup and repair, so let's get started.

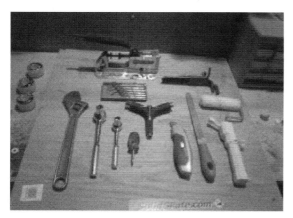

First, we need to talk about the tools you will need for assembling a skateboard. All of the tools pictured below can be used (wrench, ratchet set, screwdriver, Allen wrenches, etc.).

But the best tool for the job is going to be a skateboard tool, or skateboard wrench. It is perfect for quickly changing out the trucks, wheels, and bushings. And it is portable, so you can take it to the skatepark, and make any adjustments on site. Skate tools only cost a few bucks, so pick one up at your local skateshop. Also, we will need a razor blade, and file for installation of the griptape.

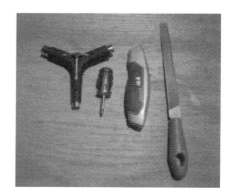

Installing the Griptape

1] Ok, before we install the griptape, we are going to lay the skateboard flat on a table.

2] Next, we are going to lay the sheet of griptape over the skateboard. Make sure it is big enough to cover the entire deck. Most sheets will be around 9" x 34". So, if you are planning on gripping a deck 9" or wider, you will need 2 sheets.

3] Notice the griptape is backed by a thick layer of paper. You will need to separate the griptape from the backing.

4] If the griptape is super sticky, you will need to be careful when removing the backing. Make sure the griptape doesn't touch anything prior to it's installation.

5] Now, place the sheet of griptape on the edge of the skateboard's nose or tail. Press down with your thumb.

6] Press down with your thumb.

7] If you have a small paint roller, roll down the middle of the deck, making sure there are no air bubbles in the griptape. Note: if there are any air bubbles left in the griptape after you have rolled the entire deck, then you can use your razor blade to puncture the griptape at that spot. Then just press down until all of the air has escaped.

8] Roll up and down the center of the deck

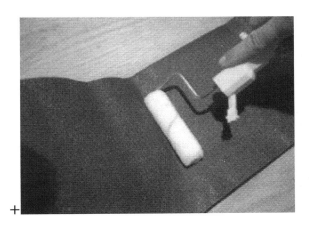

10] Then, roll the sides. Start at the center of the deck, and roll towards the edges. This will remove any air bubbles that may be left.

11] The griptape is now ready to be cut.

12] Time to cut off the excess griptape. Cut a line in the griptape perpendicular to the deck, at each of the 4 wheel wells. This will make it easier to file the edges. Once your razor blade hits the deck, stop cutting.

13] Be very careful not to let the razor blade slip and cut your hand! Don't make any fast movements, and keep all of your fingers away from the razor blade

14] Next, we are going to file around the edges of the deck.

15] Hold the file at an angle and file in one direction around the entire deck.

16] Be careful when filing over the wheel wells, where you made your initial cuts. Don't file over them too fast, or you can put a large tear in the griptape.

You want to remove the grit, so it will be easy to cut through.

17] Notice how the griptape becomes lighter in color when the grit is removed.

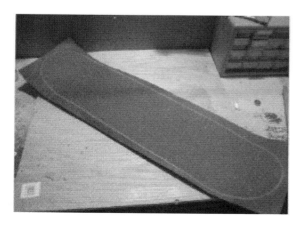

18] Next, quickly fold up the excess grip tape along the edge of the deck. This will make it easy to cut.

19] Take your razor blade and start cutting at an angle along the edges of the deck. Start at one of the four wheel well cuts you already made. Follow the white outline that you just filed. Be careful not to cut into the deck.

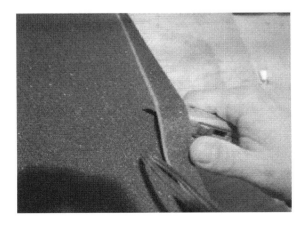

20] The deck will be your guide and will hold the razor blade in place as you move around its outline. Be careful when cutting by the wheel wells, and around the edges. If you make any mistakes, they can be fixed later.

21] Remember, if your razor blade curves into the deck, you will cut off too much griptape. If your razor blade curves away from the deck, you wont cut off enough griptape. But that can be easily filed off in the next step.

22] Save your scraps. You will need them to seal the edges.

23] Next, file around the edges of the deck. Use the flat part of the file for this. Be sure to file off any excess griptape that was not cut off before Next, file around the edges of the deck. Use the flat part of the file for this. Be sure to file off any excess griptape that was not cut

off before

24] Time to seal the edges of the griptape. Sealing the edges will keep the griptape firmly attached to your deck. This is important when your deck goes flying and scapes against the ground. If it is not sealed, then the griptape could get pulled off. Once it gets pulled off, it is harder to keep on. Grab your scraps of griptape. Use them to sand along the edges of the deck.

25] You will now notice a black outline around the griptape. This is caused by the griptape fusing with the deck.

Installing the Hardware

26] Use a small screwdriver to poke some holes in the griptape where the hardware will go through.

27] Then turn the deck over, and push your skateboard hardware through the eight holes. The bolts used in skateboard hardware can be anywhere from 3/4" long to 1.5" long. The length of the hardware will depend on whether or not you are going to use riser pads to lift up your trucks. If you are not using riser pads, then you can use 3/4" or 1" hardware, which is readily available at any skateshop. If you plan on using 1/8" riser pads, you might want to try 1" hardware.

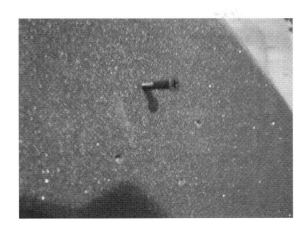

28] The length of the hardware will depend on whether or not you are going to use riser pads to lift up your trucks. If you are not using riser pads, then you can use 3/4" or 1" hardware, which is readily available at any skateshop. If you plan on using 1/8" riser pads, you might want to try 1" hardware.

29] If you are riding on 60mm wheels, you might want to try 1/4" riser pads and 1" hardware. If you are riding 65mm wheels or bigger, then you will want 1/2" to 1" riser pads and 1.5" hardware. Note: you will also need to take into consideration the thickness of the truck baseplate. This will also help determine the size of the hardware and risers that you need. Thicker baseplates require longer hardware

Installing the Riser Pads

30] Next, if you are going to use riser pads, place them on the bolts now. You will notice there are two sets of holes in the riser pads, one for old school bolt patterns and one for new school bolt pattners. The old school bolt patterns are the holes that are farthest apart from each other. If you have an old set of skateboard trucks from the 1980's, then it will probably have the old bolt pattern.

31] But if you have newer trucks, they will have the smaller, new school bolt pattern. Note: some trucks will be equipped with the new and old bolt patterns. The typical skateboard deck manufactured today will be drilled for the new school bolt pattern.

Installing the Trucks

32] Now you are ready to place the trucks on the deck. Next, put the nuts on the bolts.

33] Tighten them by hand.

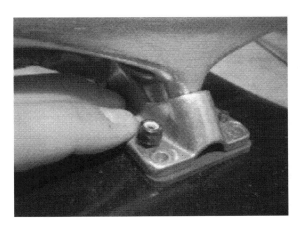

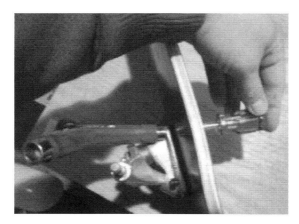

34] Next, tighten the four bolts with your skate tool. Tighten the bolts that are diagonal to each other first.

Never tighten the two bolts closest to the tail, or the two bolts closest to the nose first. This can cause the deck to crack, if too much force is applied on only one side of the baseplate.

35] Don't over-tighten the hardware. You want the heads of the bolts to be flush with the top of the skateboard deck.

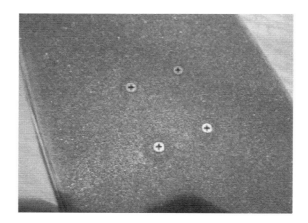

Be Careful

If you tighten the bolts too much, the bolt heads will sink down into the deck. The excess force will crush the wood fibers. This will cause the deck to fatigue much quicker. I overtightened skateboard hardware in the past and have cracked decks in a matter of minutes. If the trucks are tightened properly, the baseplate will not move when you try to wiggle it.

Installing the Wheels and Bearings

36] We will be installing FKD bearings with neoprene shields on this skateboard. Notice the kit comes with 8 bearings and 4 spacers to stick inside each wheel.

37] First, you are going to push the bearing into the wheel with your hand. It may only go in a little bit depending on the size of the wheel.

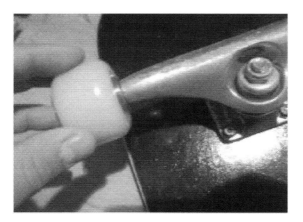

38] Next, place the wheel on the truck axle, and give it another good push.

You want the bearing touching the truck hanger. In other words, when you give it a push, the truck hanger will force the bearing into the wheel. Notice how the bearing is now in the wheel.

Install Bearing Spacers

39] Now let's put the bearing spacer inside the wheel. These keep the wheel and bearings locked into a tight position, which will add performance and reliability to the bearings.

If spacers are not applied to the wheels, then the bearings can make lateral movements on the axle. If you are doing a big trick and land on a crooked wheel, then bearing damage can occur to one or more of the bearings, or to the cage or shield. Also, some skaters believe that spacers make the bearings roll faster, because of a decreased loss of energy, and a better fit on the axle. I can't really tell a difference, but I'm sure spacers do help, at least a little bit. If you plan on going very fast on your skateboard, then you should probably pick up some spacers.

40]  **41]**

In other words, you can put the wheel and bearings on the axle and tighten the bolt enough to force the bearings inside the wheel. Just be careful not to damage the bearing shield, or the part that actually protects the ball bearings. Metal shields can dent very easily. I prefer neoprene shields. Neoprene shields can flex, and they are easy to take off. When a metal shield is dented or damaged, its only a matter of time before it falls off.

42] Now install the bearing on the other side. Throw a thin washer on the axle, then place the wheel on the axle. Place another thin washer on the axle. Washers on either side of the bearings will help keep dirt out, and also keep the shields from falling off.

43] Note: if you placed the wheel and washers on the axle, and there are not enough threads left on the axle to screw down the nut, then the bearings will need to be pushed further inside the wheel.

44] To do this, take one of the washers off. Then place the nut on the axle.

45] Screw it down enough so that the wheel can barely spin.

Then loosen the nut, and reinstall the wheel and washers like normal.

46] Now that the wheel is on the axle, and enough axle threads are visible, we are going to tighten the axle bolt with the skate tool.

Tighten it enough so that the wheel cannot move up and down on the axle.

47] There should be a little bit of lateral movement left in the wheel, and the wheel should spin freely for a few seconds when you give it a good turn.

Note: some skaters like to tighten the wheels even more when using bearings spacers inside the wheel, eliminating all lateral movement. In this case, the wheel will only spin a few turns before stopping, but will still roll fast when in use. This will keep the bearings and wheels in perfect allignment, which is important if you are into downhill longboarding, street luge or slalom.

48] Note: some skaters like to tighten the wheels even more when using bearings spacers inside the wheel, eliminating all lateral movement. In this case, the wheel will only spin a few turns before stopping, but will still roll fast when in use. This will keep the bearings and wheels in perfect allignment, which is important if you are into downhill longboarding, street luge or slalom.

Using a Bearing Press

49]
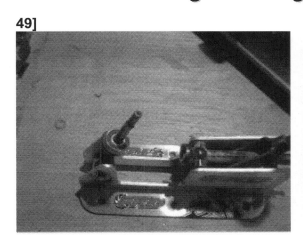

50]

If you are lucky enough to have a bearing press, then installing bearings and spacers is a breeze. Just put the parts on the press axle, and crank the arm to push everything together. Great for making quick changes. These sell for about $25 on Ebay and are well worth the money.

51]

52]

Adjusting the Trucks

We are almost finished. All we have left to do is adjust the truck bushings. The bushings are the urethane objects that control how the axle will move.

Most new trucks will need to have their bushings tightened, unless you prefer loose trucks. Loose trucks are great for turning and carving, but are also unstable at high speeds and on transitions.

So if you have very loose trucks, you can lose your balance, and usually at the worst possible time. Loose trucks can also slow down a skateboard, since they are better equipped to absorb the energy that would normally get transformed to the wheels.

Likewise, if you tighten your trucks too much, you will not be able to turn effectively, and the skateboard will only go straight. This can be just as bad. On another note, tighter trucks can make your skateboard go faster, since less energy is transformed into the bushings.

Also, tighter trucks can make tech skateboarding tricks, like kickflips and 360 flips, easier to perform because more energy can be transformed into flipping the board around. If you only skate street, and don't visit skateparks often, then tighter trucks might be for you.

For most skaters, however, the best option is a medium truck tightness. Medium trucks will give you optimal board control, while allowing the trucks to turn fully.

53] This truck needs to be adjusted to a medium tightness. The Kingpin bolt (the bolt that tightens the bushings) has only been hand tightened. Most new trucks will be sold like this.

54] Use your skate tool to tighten the kingpin bolt, the biggest bolt on the truck. Give it a few full turns, and check the tightness. Use your hand to push one of the wheels towards the deck. It should be hard to do, but possible.

55] The wheel should not touch the deck. If you can push it to the deck, you might need to tighten the bushings more.

Next, stand on the skateboard and see how trucks feel. You should be able to turn easily, while maintaining balance and control.

It will take some time before you know the perfect bushing tightness, so be patient.

Note: bushings can come in different hardnesses. This complicates things a bit more. Harder bushings will need to be tightened less and softer bushings will need to be tightened more.

Most of the bushings sold today are considered medium hardness.

56] The truck at the right uses an inverted kingpin, or upside-down kingpin. This allows for a lower kingpin height, and a smoother grind.

You will need to use an Allen wrench to adjust trucks like these.

Break In Your Skateboard.

Be sure to break in your skateboard before hitting the skateparks or any type of dangerous terrain. Get used to how the skateboard feels and how it turns.

Also, learn how to fall down properly.

Always wear a helmet.

The bottom line is that you are going to fall. It's a part of skateboarding. So always wear a helmet to protect your head. There are many cool helmets out on the market today. They are lightweight and have air vents to dissipate heat.

✓ Stop by your local skateshop and pick up a good helmet today.

Some Common Skateboard Repairs

Changing the Griptape

Griptape will eventually wear out and need to be replaced. Just like sandpaper, the grit will fall off, and the griptape will smoothen out. When this happens, you won't have enough traction, and your feet will slip off of the skateboard deck.

This might not sound like a big deal, but if you are skating pretty fast, it could be very dangerous. If your front foot slips off and lands in front of your moving skateboard, you are looking at a sprained, or even broken, ankle.

Always keep extra griptape around because you will definitely need it. To remove the old griptape, you will need to use a razor blade. Push the razor blade underneath the old griptape and lift it up. Then use your hand to pull the old griptape off.

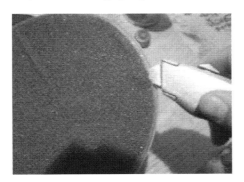

57] To remove the old griptape, you will need to use a razor blade. Push the razor blade underneath the old griptape and lift it up. Then use your hand to pull the old griptape off.

58] Be very careful not to let the razor blade slip and cut your hand! Don't make any fast movements, and keep all of your fingers away from the razor blade.

Cleaning the Bearings

59] First make sure the shields are removable. If they are not, you will have to spray the bearings with a good aerosol lubricant like Tri-Flow to remove the dirt, contaminants, and moisture. Just give the bearings a good spray and you're done.

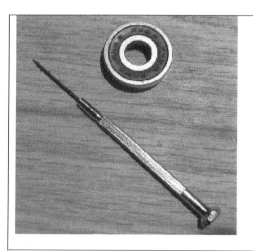

60] If the bearings have removable shields, you will need to use a small screwdriver to pry out the shield.

61] Note: some metal shields have a small c-ring that needs to be pried out first before you can remove the shield. Getting the c-rings out is a huge pain, and can result in shield damage. If you have c-rings on your bearings, you might want to just spray them with Tri-Flow.

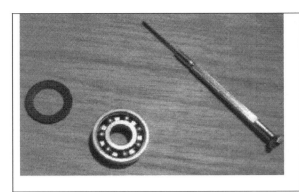

62] If you have c-rings on your bearings, you might want to just spray them with Tri-Flow or use "Sonic" Citrus Bearing cleaner.

Ultra-cleaning the Bearings

63] If you want to get the bearings super clean, soak them for a while in a good biodegradeable cleaner, like Simple Green.

Or, you can try "Sonic" Citrus Bearing cleaner.

Just throw the bearings in a jar or bottle, add the cleaner, and shake like crazy.

If the bearings are still dirty after cleaning them, you might want to get out a toothbrush and give them a thorough brushing.

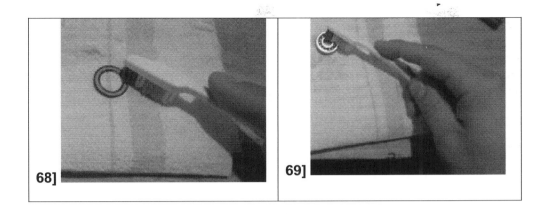

Then, it's back to the "Simple Green".

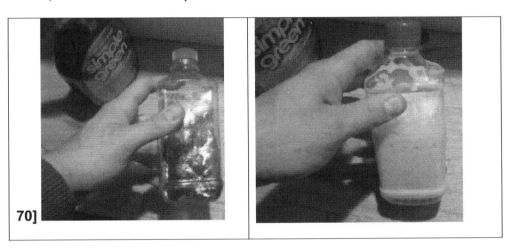

Now, it's time to dry and lube them.

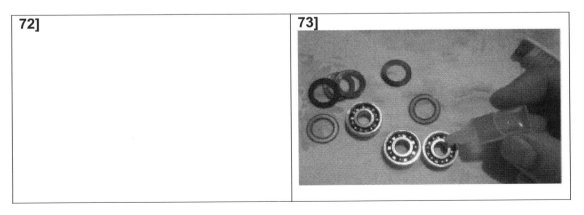

Snap the shields back into position.

74] Snap the shields back into position.

75] The bearings are now ready to ride.

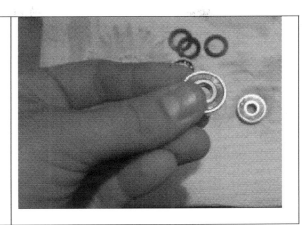

Choosing and Using Lubricants

Once you are done cleaning the bearings, let them dry and lube them up with your favorite lubricant.

Heavier lubricants like grease or cream do a good job of protecting the bearings and keeping out dirt, but they will make the bearings roll a little slower.

The lighter oil lubricants and speed lubes will allow the bearings to roll faster, but need to be maintained more often than the grease or cream.

If you really want your bearings to roll super fast, use a spray lubricant that comes in an aerosol can. Your bearings will need to be cleaned every few days because the lightest lubricants, like WD-40, leak out of the bearings. But, they will roll fast.

Now, snap the shields back and you're *ready to roll*.

If you don't have Simple Green or Citrus Cleaner, you can always use a solvent like paint thinner to clean your bearings. Pretty much every garage on the world has a container of paint thinner hidden in it somewhere.

> Be careful with any solvents you touch; they can be very flammable and irritate the skin. The spray aerosols can leave a sticky film on your bearings, which can attract dirt.

With that being said, some skaters still swear by WD-40 as the best lubricant.

There are even some skaters out there that refuse to use any lubrication at all on their bearings. While this might get your bearings rolling faster than the speed of light, it will eventually lead to them falling apart. I personally never clean or lube my bearings and I think my skateboard rolls pretty darn quick. However, if I get any moisture in the bearings, they tend to lock up from rust.

So, if you don't clean or lube your bearings, always have a spare set handy.

Changing the Kingpin Bushings and Pivot Bushing

If you need to keep tightening your bushings every few weeks, then its probably time to change them out. To do this, remove the kingpin bolt.

76]

77]

Next, wiggle the truck hanger until it loosens up and can be removed from the kingpin.

78] Next, wiggle the truck hanger until it loosens up and can be removed from the kingpin.

Now you can switch out the bushings, and install the truck hanger back on the kingpin.

79] The bigger bushing goes on the bottom, and the smaller bushing goes on top.

Then put the kingpin bolt back on and tighten it to the desired bushing stiffness.

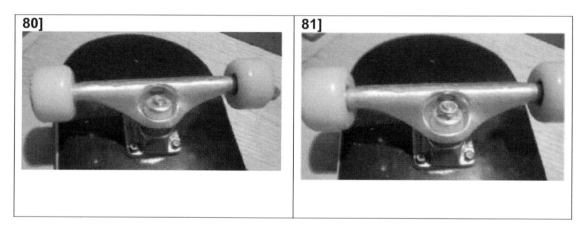

80]

81]

Replacing the Small Pivot Bushing

If you need to replace the small pivot bushing, pry it out with a screwdriver. You might have to dig into the urethane to get it out. Then, just push the new bushing back in.

82]	83]

Changing the Kingpin

Sometimes kingpins break, or the threads get stripped. If you don't want to fork out the money for a new set of trucks, you can change out the kingpin. Simply hammer it out, and hammer the new one back in. Note: if your kingpin doesn't leave you enough room to just hammer it out on a flat surface, then place it in a vice. If you don't have a vice, lean it against a curb and hammer away. Be careful not to smash your fingers with the hammer.

84]

85]

86]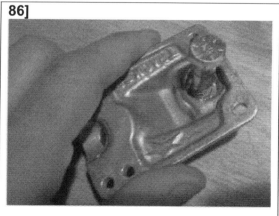

87]

If you have a vice, you can do it this way

88-90] If you have a vice, you can do it this way

88]

89]

90]

Install the New Kingpin.

Now, install the new kingpin.

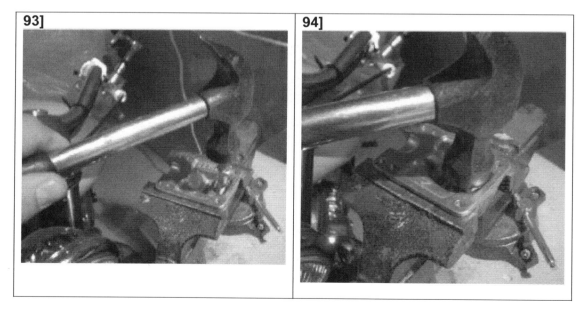

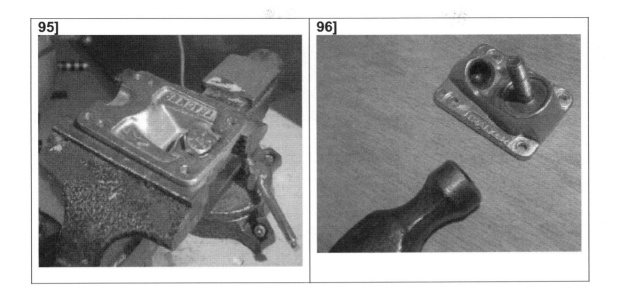

Replacing a Kingpin Without a Vice

No vice, no worries. All you need is a hammer.

No vice?

No worries! All you need is a hammer.

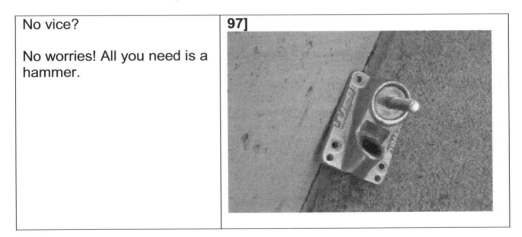

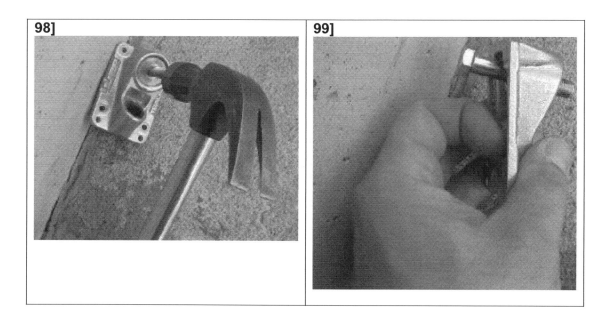

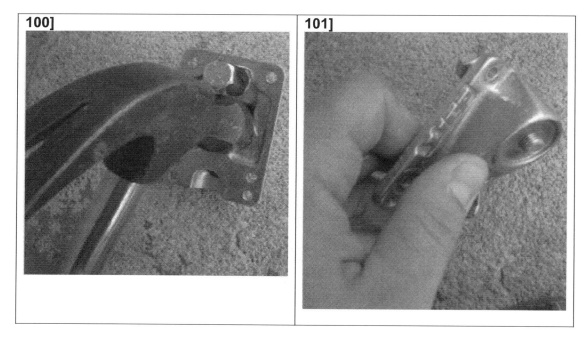

Now, all you have to do is pull out the kingpin with your hand.

Then, hammer in the new one and you are done.

Great Answers to Common Questions.

What types of varnishes do skateboard decks have?

I use the term 'varnish' to mean all kinds of clear protective coatings. Fade protection, stain protection. These are the reasons you will probably want to cover your deck with varnish, either shortly after completion.

The most common question about fading is assuming it looks good to begin with.

Here is my opinion on the matter. As a general rule;

- most latex-type paints last a few years before they begin to fade
- decks painted with good oil based paint, heat transfers or a silk screening process will last dozens of years
- all painted decks will begin to deteriorate immediately!

If it's indoors or in a cave, it'll last a lot longer if it has a coating of varnish.

If the wall traps moisture or faces the sun, you face a challenge: it will probably either fade or fall to bits (or both!) before you are done appreciating it.

This decay may be put off decades if you have the patience and commitment to take every available precaution. If it's really important to you that the graphics last forever, choose a wall that is protected from moisture and weather and sun and earthquakes, vandalism, politics and grime.

The sun's rays, in both the ultraviolet (UV) and the visible parts of the spectrum, can deteriorate and fade your paint. There are three types of deterioration which result in fading: pigment breakdown, binder breakdown, and varnish breakdown.

The first, pigment breakdown, is a chemical change in the pigments. The best protection against this is to use well formulated and richly pigmented paints.

The second, binder breakdown, can also be minimized with the right paints but, eventually, the medium that holds the pigment in place will probably dry up and become "dusty" as the medium crumbles on a microscopic level. This can be slowed by the use of a varnish protective coat. Most varnishes protect the surface of the wood from deterioration due to those nasty rays from the sun.

The third kind of "fading" is actually due to the varnish, rather than the mural paint, becoming cloudy, thus obscuring the wood's surface. This happens when UV rays break up the varnish itself, possibly by internal reflection within the varnish layer, as purposely occurs in an optical fiber. It appears that the best way to avoid this problem is to avoid putting decks with permanent urethane varnishes on walls that get a lot of sun exposure.

Other types of varnish may eventually suffer the same deterioration and clouding, but are easier to 'consolidate' when crumbled and, most important to art conservation, are much easier to remove than urethane. New paint over urethane also has limited adhesion, in case you plan to paint over it (with another?) some day.

Stain protection is just a simple matter of putting a protective coat between the sources of potential stains and the graphics itself. If the stain can't be removed, then the varnish probably can (unless you used urethane) and will probably take the stain away with it.

Some stains can't be fully removed, either because it is somehow especially potent or because of a long delay between when the stain comes calling and its attempted removal (the marker or spray paint will cure and become more permanent).

Choosing Among Varnish Products

There are at least four kinds of varnishes that stand a chance of protecting your graphics. Two are urethanes: water-based urethane and one based on petroleum distillate solvents. The other two are waxes and certain acrylics.

Some varnishes are "permanent," notably the urethanes. The others are referred to as "sacrificial" varnishes.

URETHANE: There are three main arguments against urethane:

1. It's really not permanent after all, especially when exposed to direct sunlight on a daily basis or if there's moisture seeping into the wood from behind the graphics.

2. There's the occasional problem of "ambering" (darkening or yellowing) that most urethanes have to some extent, even the ones that claim otherwise.

3. A urethane covered deck can be impossible to repair after it is damaged by any of those processes.

ACRYLIC POLYMERS: One technique that comes highly recommended is an acrylic varnish. That is because acrylic on its own can absorb grime, fumes and dust in its pores. Acrylic polymers also can be good on their own, serving as something midway between a fully sacrificial varnish and a permanent protective film. If your reaction time is within a week, you can remove most stains very easily without the varnish coming off. But, if you need to remove a more stubborn stain you can, with a lot of work, soften the varnish with solvents and treat it as sacrificial.

The Varnish We Chose

The varnish for our project was some type of acrylic, though the "trade secret" formula and the non-chemist sales folk made it impossible to get some of the facts. The product we used is a two-part (like many urethanes and epoxies), water-based, acrylic co-polymer. You can brush it on, roll it on or spray it on.

We have experienced only one problem with our varnish: crazing. This is when the gradual shrinkage of the varnish film leaves micro gaps, in an alligator-skin that is pattern barely visible to the naked eye. Sometimes, after cleaning, there's still a very slightly darker area because of the stains in the tiny cracks (it requires a really close look).

We plan to fix that problem before long by reapplying a coat of the varnish or a solvent that "remelts" and uncrazes the varnish.

As I implied, there are two approaches to fixing the crazed pattern: apply another coat or two to fill the wee gaps or - a more enduring option - redissolve the surface and make a continuous film layer again.

Inspect the wood, regularly. Sand any nicks or splintering. Refinish with Varathane or Spar Varnish as needed. Left untreated, they allow moisture to permeate the wood, which will eventually weaken the wood.

Finishing

Many decks come with a single coat of Varathane or Spar Varnish. This first coat seals the wood and makes the wood a little harder, and helps it to resist wear. Adding additional coats of either varnish or paint will increase wear-resistance and protection from the elements.

If you decide to add additional finish yourself, there are a few things you should know:

- Ideally, you should lightly sand and coat all the wood with Varathane or Spar Varnish for at least three layers - four or five would be best.

- You must lightly sand between each application using 300 grit paper.

- Several layers of Spar Varnish or Varathane make the wood look REALLY nice.

- You can expect this process to take several days, however, since you must wait for each coat to dry. Or you can apply any sturdy paint of your choice.

How can graphics and finishes affect a skateboard's performance?

Have you ever wondered why one type of deck slides better than another, or why some skaters prefer blanks over graphic decks? The chemicals and inks applied to a board can make a difference and should be considered each time you buy a deck.

Heat Transfers

The most economical option for manufacturers involves using the Heat Tranfer method. This process is similar to the application of iron-on graphics that are widely used in the t-shirt industry. Although Heat Transfers cost next to nothing to make, they can wear down rather quickly and flake off. They also lack the vivid colors that most consumers desire. Heat Transfer sheets can, though, add thousands of colors to a deck's graphic without the added labor expenses. The low cost of the transfer, application process, and labor makes the Heat Transfer process the skateboard industry's best choice for cutting costs and staying competitive.

Silk-Screening

Silk-screening is the process of using a frame, ink, and squeegee to apply deck graphics. Most companies that silk-screen their decks use water based paints, due to the environmental restrictions placed on all other types of ink.

Although silk-screened decks can look appealing, the artistic extent of the designer is minimized due to the limitations inherit to this process. Increased labor cost is one major factor, which can detract from this method. Another is turnaround time. The process of silk screening can even add another week to the manufacturing process to allow for increased drying times.

Silk-screened decks tend to be more resistant to wear and tear than heat transfer decks, but are not as durable as the UV painted decks. Silk screening costs can range from $0.60 to $1.00 per color, depending on the quantity ordered from the manufacturer.

Silk-screen painted decks slide well and look great, but are probably on their way out, as their high cost is prohibitive.

Ultra Violet Painting

Companies such as California Skate Factory are using a process called Ultra Violet Painting. The UV ink is actually baked into the bottom of the deck during this process, increasing deck longevity. This method uses less ink, which results in less weight and lower costs. UV coatings last up to 40% longer than silk-screened graphics and 80% longer than Heat Transfer graphics. This process is also very quick, preventing the decks from drying out during the painting process. If you are a consumer, then all you need to know is that this UV stuff is good.

Clear Coating

After the painting is completed, a sealing coat is applied followed up by a clear coat to protect the graphics and increase the deck's ability to resist abrasion. For the most part, clear coating is applied to all decks, whether they use water based paint, silk screens, UV paint or Heat Transfers.

Some companies do, however, cut costs by deleting this process. Unfortunately, doing so can make a deck wear prematurely.

SST Coating

An interesting side-note is the use of a special coating called SST by Skate One. The Powell Mini Logo SST coating helps the deck perform better and slide faster while extending deck life. SST is something that most skaters don't really appreciate, even though it is worth checking out.

Shrink Wrap

Shrink wrap is a vital part of board preservation. It allows the ink some time to cure and prevents excessive moisture swings during the shipping process. Shrink wrap application adds about $0.25 to the packaging process.

Summary

We have a winner. The best coating comes from the UV Process. SST coatings rate high, but are not as thick as the UV coatings and will not last quite as long.

When considering skateboard deck concaves, how steep is too steep?

Have you noticed how steep some concaves have become?

Some companies are even giving the deep concave designs fancy names to aid in the marketing of their 'new and improved' product.

Some concave will definitely improve performance. But, there is a point where - if it is too steep - it can hinder a deck's performance. A deck with a really steep concave is often too stiff for the average rider.

Then, why are they making them so steep? Well, concave adds a lot of strength. However, some manufacturers offset this because they use inferior materials, and rely only on deck design.

So, more concave does not always mean more strength. Plus, a deck with a steeper concave is a little harder to ride, and some riders complain about not being able to keep their feet positioned on the deck.

Another problem is that the wood is being pressed together at 25,000 to 30,000 psi to achieve these deep concaves. The high pressure may damage wood fibers, resulting in a shorter deck life.

And, many manufactures are pressing molds with 8-10 decks at a time. The decks in the center of the mold are usually the ones that have issues. They tend to not have the same shape and performance as the decks pressed closer to the ends of the mold. The center decks don't get an even pressure, resulting in early deck fatigue.

So, how steep is too steep? It is really just a matter of personal preference. Think of it like this. A deck acts like a spring. Weight, force, and energy are applied, causing it to flex. If you are light, it will be harder to get any real response from a stiff deck. If your skateboard is springy, then you may need a thicker deck, or one with a steeper concave.

Let's not forget about the problem with inferior materials, because this really complicates the matter.

Bottom line, if the wood is good, a steep concave will definitely be stronger. But, it will be harder to skate if it is too steep.

If the wood is junk, a steep concave will still add strength. But, it will not be any stronger than an average deck with a mellow concave.

Can you tell me something I don't already know about skateboard decks?

Why is Maple the Best Choice?

Maple is used in the construction process are because of price, strength, weight, availability, split resistance and hardness. Maple is a hardwood which comes from deciduous trees (trees that loose their leaves each year during cooler months). Oak and Walnut make up half of all hardwood production. Other trees that are used include Beech, Birch, Cherry, Elm, Gum, and Hickory.

What is the Best Maple Skateboard deck on the market?

Good question, but hard to answer.

After testing hundreds of decks, I am a little apprehensive to pick just one. There are some great decks on the market today, and no single one deck will fit everyone's needs.

Some people like a stiffer deck, based on skill level, weight, and the type of skating they do. Others prefer a more flexible deck.

During my testing, I sought out decks that were not too stiff, or too flexible, more middle of the road types.

Decks manufactured by CSF and Performance SK8 are very good. Dykema, Jart, Penn's Wood, Baker, Powell, Watson Laminates and Acme would also be very good choices.

Another recommendation is to try out someone else's skateboard to get a feel for the different sizes, shapes, and concaves available.

Good luck!

What Makes a Board Pop Good?

Design, moisture content, compound curves, core heights, cure times and temperatures, nature of adhesives, mode of curing, tightness of veneer cut, grain direction, tightness of grain and orientation of grain all affect board pop.

If moisture content is too high, the board will be too flexible.

If moisture content is too low, the board won't bend - it will break!

How Does Moisture Content Affect Strength?

Moisture content greatly affects board life. The higher the moisture content, the weaker the board.

For example, 6-12% is needed to ensure that the laminating process will hold the wood together properly. Some companies drop the moisture content to 5-6% to ensure that the laminating process is completed properly. Lowering the moisture montent can ensure long board life and decrease shipping costs.

Improperly stored decks also contribute to premature weakness. Wood should be dried at the same moisture content (MC) as the environment it is intended to occupy.

The relative humidity in most homes averages around 30 to 40%. This equals 6-7% equilibrium moisture content.

Wood is constantly adjusting to its environment. It is continually gaining and losing moisture from the air around it. Even after wood has dried to the proper moisture content, its Moisture Content can change during storage, manufacturing or use.

Design also plays a major role in performance and personal preference.

Why Do Boards Chip, Delaminate, and Snap in Half?

An unpopular deck that sits on the store shelf for two to three years will, in fact, become stronger and less flexible than its newer counterparts. This is the result of an acclimated moisture content.

For example, I purchased 10 WalMart X2S decks recently for stress testing. The reasons that they had not sold (possibly poor appearance and construction) contributed to their improved performance.

Although this doesn't address the design aspects of these decks, it does explain why they performed better that some of the popular decks.

Any wood fatigues more quickly when moisture levels are high.

How is a Skateboard Made?

The first step in making a skateboard is choosing the desired Maple tree. The finest Canadian Hardrock Maple comes from the Great Lakes Region in North America. The Maple from this area is known for its tight wood grain and superior strength.

After the trees are cut down and stripped, they are divided into thin veneers.

7 plys of Maple are then prepared for the laminating and adhesive process. Each veneer is fed through a gluing machine that applies a thin layer of glue.

After the glue has been applied, the veneers are put into a hydraulic press, which forms the nose, tail, and concave of the board. The result is a seven-ply skateboard deck, made from 4 horizontal plys and 3 vertical plys, although some companies use 5 horizontal plys and 2 vertical plys.

After the board is out of the press, it is ready to be cut. The molded blanks are then drilled for the desired wheel base.

After that, the skateboards are shaped using a band saw.

Next, the decks are sprayed with a sealant.

They are now ready for the graphics to be applied. After the boards have been printed, they are stacked in racks.

Once dry, the decks are boxed up and shipped out to all the local skateboard shops.

Will the skateboarding industry quit using wood and start using more composites?

The glues, paints, adhesives, epoxy and resins used in the manufacture of skateboards have been receiving attention for years. The future of skateboarding will probably have wood-composite mixtures, which will eventually edge out the traditional wood deck market.

New and exciting products, such as carbon, fiberglass, aluminum, plastic, and even bamboo, are receiving increased attention.

The downside is, some of these materials are just as environmentally unsound as cutting down trees. Epoxy and resins produce a large amount of waste that requires special handling and disposal, not to mention the health problems associated with working with these chemicals.

But, if you want to build a better mouse trap, all avenues must be explored.

Why do some decks delaminate?

Delamination is a big concern for skaters, retailers and manufacturers alike. This growing problem is actually the result of some of the recent changes in the skateboard industry. An increasingly profit-driven environment has caused a few of the major manufacturers to skimp on wood and glue quality, drying times and manufacturing processes.

Plus, an increase in global competition has left some tough choices for everyone.

Drying Times

Back to the drying times. Basically, if the wood is not dried to a low enough moisture content (3-6% depending on the wood and glue process), it will not hold together. If the wood is only surface dried, or it is dried to a point where it has a high moisture content when the deck is constructed, it will expand and contract considerably. Too much, in fact, for the glue to remain an effective bond.

The plys of wood in a skateboard have the unique characteristic of maintaining the same properties relative to the moisture level they were initially dried at. If you only partially dry wood, it will gain additional moisture. Much more, in fact, than wood dried at a lower moisture level.

The end result is a lack of strength. Wood at a 16% moisture content is only half as strong as wood at a 2-3% moisture content.

Pressing the Wood

Let's talk about the pressing process.

If too many decks are pressed in a single mold, shape will vary from deck to deck. This contributes to deck failure, due to improper design characteristics and an irregular, uneven compression placed on each wood layer.

Some companies use an excessive force during compression to offset this problem. However, this can result in substantial wood fiber damage which will cause premature fatigue.

There is a problem where some companies rely too much on deck design to increase strength. Deeper deck concaves alone can't correct this problem. Once a deck is stressed, it can still delaminate and lose its performance characteristics, even with a special concave design.

Glue Use

Inexpensive glues are used to decrease costs and often, the companies pass on some of those savings to consumers in lower prices. There are a few high quality glues currently in use in the USA. Although using a reputable glue requires more time for production, it also allows for a decrease in environmental restrictions. Environmental issues in the USA have caused many companies to seek environmentally friendly alternatives to the once standard glues on the market.

In fact, those older types of glue still plague the industry, and their clean up will continue to haunt the industry for years to come.

Some USA companies are seeking to move overseas to avoid the environmental restrictions. This is also partly profit-driven. Once the bean counters start taking over skateboard manufacturing, the problems we see today will start showing up more frequently. Other issues, such as labor costs, workers compensation, unemployment, retirement, insurance, competition and taxes can also put pressure on companies to move overseas while trying to keep their heads above water.

When do I need to use riser pads?

Ever since risers have been on the market, the average kid has wondered when getting that first skateboard, "Why is this on my deck and do I need it?"

Well, I too have fallen victim to this problem. First of all, I use them. I guess it goes a little beyond my desire to not have the wheels rub the bottom of my deck (which causes flat spots on the wheels, giving a rougher ride and shorting wheel life) and marking up the deck.

It is more to do with the truck itself being bolted to the bottom of my deck. The truck base can and does make a impression on the bottom of the deck when mounted without risers.

So What!? Well, this impression is damaging the deck wood fibers and making the deck weaker, thus shortening deck life. The riser also acts like a shock absorber, the same as the bushings on the trucks and the wheels. Energy is absorbed by them and it makes for a smoother ride.

The kingpin from some trucks can also damage the deck. Most decks fatigue along the truck base, either in front or behind the truck, depending on the tricks you do and how you ride most often.

I call it the Fault Line.

Risers generally range from 1/8"-1/2" thick.

Riser hardness is also a big topic with some skaters. Again, the type of skating you do changes your performance needs. The harder risers are better for tricks, and the softer risers are better for cruising and preventing deck fatigue.

Which Bearings are Better; ABEC 3, ABEC 5 or ABEC 7?

Some of the first bearings used for skateboards were actually adapted from vacuum cleaners.

The bearings you see on the market today are sealed precision bearings, of standard size and width, rated by the Annular Bearing Engineering Committee.

Although most bearings do not require additional lubrication and are maintenance free, they do fail. The seals tend to get water and dirt in them, and this shortens bearing life.

The bearing rating system in use today is really for machinery, and not very effective for rating skateboard bearings. So, the ABEC rating doesn't mean much, unless you plan on skating 50 mph.

The more precise the bearings are, the shorter their life span.

A bearing rated at ABEC 7, although faster, may not last as long as an ABEC 3 bearing, due to fact that it is more susceptible to wear and tear caused by a close, more precise tolerance.

For example, look at the old school bearings from the 1970's. If maintained, they could probably last forever. They were just a couple of ball bearings held together by 2 shields. The tolerances back then were not precise at all. The ball bearings were not constantly in contact with cages and shields and a core to hold them in perfect allignment.

In fact, some of those bearings were not in contact at all, and would fall out while skating!

They might be able to last forever, but there is a downside. Those bearings always got dirt and water in them, and needed continuous maintenance.

I admit it is hard to resist the faster bearings, but after a few days of skating, it's really hard to tell them apart from the ABEC 3 bearings. The best advice is to try different types out for yourself, and if you really want to spend a lot of money, buy a good set of Rocket ceramic bearings from RockinRon. These will set you back about $100. The ceramic balls in these types of bearings are lighter, stronger and very precise. The steel balls in most cheaper bearings are not perfectly round and can even get dents, dings, or pits from use.

A smooth ceramic ball is much closer to a perfect circle, and can roll much faster.

What Kind of Wheels are Best for Skateboarding?

Skateboard wheels have changed a lot over the years. During the 50's, steel wheels were the norm. They were tough, rode even rougher and offered very little traction or board control.

By 1960, clay wheels were invented. But like metal wheels, they lacked the control and performance desired by skateboarders.

Then, in the 70's, Frank Nasworthy adapted urethane wheels from rollerskates. Urethane wheels offer great traction, abrasion resistance and rebound quickly. Also, urethane is naturally clear in color.

Keep in mind that color additives can weaken the wheels and shorten their lifespan.

The key to selecting the right wheel depends on the type of skating that you want to do. Don't worry too much about the brand of the wheels. There are only a few factories that make all of the skateboard wheels in the world, so a bunch of different companies sell the exact same skateboard wheel, with just different graphics on them.

The biggest factor to consider is probably going to be size. Smaller wheels are lightweight and designed for street skating, while large wheels are designed for park and ramp skating.

The really big wheels, 70mm to 100mm, are designed for downhill longboarding and street luge. The durometer measures the wheel hardness. The average durometer for a skateboard wheel is 97A-99A. The smaller the number, the softer the wheel. Also, the higher the letter, the harder the wheel. A 97B wheel is harder than a 97A wheel.

Larger wheels are softer by design and tend to give a smoother ride. These wheels usually have a harder core inside them which protects the bearing.

- For transition and vertical skating, try a 78A-98A wheel hardness with a 54mm-65mm wheel size.

- For street and technical skating, try a 98A-100A hardness with a 50mm-52mm wheel size.

- For general skating (street and park), try a 95A-100A hardness with a a 52mm-54mm size.

- If you want to ride a longboard that is 36" to 42" long, try a 78A-80A hardness with a 65mm-70mm wheel.

Soft wheels like 78A's are very comfortable. They absorb a tremendous amount of vibration, and you feel like you can ride over anything on them. Definitely worth trying out. The only downside is, they are pretty heavy. Bigger wheels like these will also need bigger risers pads to prevent wheel bite. Wheel bite is caused by the wheel touching the bottom of the deck during a turn. It is a bad, bad thing.

Remember, skateboard trucks turn by bringing the axle closer to the deck, and by shortening the wheelbase on two of the four wheels. So, if the trucks turn enough to cause the wheels to touch the deck, then your skateboard will stop suddenly, and you will go flying off your board.

Keep in mind, the bigger the wheels, the bigger the riser pads.

Step on your board and see if the wheels touch the deck when you lean to one side. If they do, then you need to add bigger riser pads.

Risers come in a bunch of different sizes, so it's easy to find the perfect height needed. They come in 1/8", 1/4", 1/2", and 1". So if you are riding 70mm wheels and need 3/4" risers, just stack a 1/2" on top of a 1/4" riser pad.

Note: wheelbase can also determine the proper riser pad size. If you are skating a bigger deck, like a 36" one with a 15" wheelbase, then it can bottom out when riding over skatepark coping while doing certain tricks, like a rock to fakie.

So, if you don't want the center of the deck to get stuck on the coping, just add some risers to jack up the trucks.

The normal skateboard deck wheelbase is 14" for a deck length of 31" to 32.5". However, decks longer than 32" often have longer wheelbases. A longer wheelbase adds more stability and control and is great for taller riders. It can also slow you down a bit on transitions.

It really all adds up to personal preference.

How Do I Break My Bearings in?

SKATE, SKATE, SKATE. The ABEC bearings will be a little faster to begin with but, due to the close tolerances of the bearings, they will slow down, or wear in, after a few days or weeks of skating.

To be honest, unless you have tons of cash, don't waste your time buying super expensive bearings, unless your into downhill or slalom.

Just be sure to keep an eye on your bearings from time to time. If a bearing separates or wears out, replace it or (for greater safety) the whole set.

What Kind of Wheel Lubricant Should I Buy for my Bearings?

How many of you actually lubricate your bearings?

I recently discussed this with a group of skaters and the response varied.

So, I tested a few to get a feel for how lubrication affects speed and performance. The ones I tested were motor oil, graphite, grease, WD-40 and some oil-based spray lubricants.

The test was not too scientific. I just applied different lubricants over time to different skateboards, skated them and wrote down the results, which are kind of surprising.

The cheapest oil-based lubricant from Wal-Mart was actually the best one. So, if you have a need for speed, just lubricate often, and use an oil-based lubricant.

What are the Best Bearings to Skate with?

The best bearings to skate with are the ones that roll nicely. ABEC ratings are nothing but a gimmick and deal mainly with electric motors. Seeing that we don't skate motors, the only thing the ABEC rating truly means is price. Granted, the higher rated bearings might feel smoother, but they really aren't.

I have tried ABEC 3's, 5's, 7's and 9's and I skated fast on all of them. Then, there are the 9 ball bearings. Now, if you can find these, especially ceramic ones, then by all means pick them up. Ceramic does not crush, or pit like metal and the weight is more evenly distributed, making these puppies strong.

How do Trucks Work?

Skateboard trucks were introduced in the early 1970's, just after the invention of the urethane wheel. Before that, roller skate assemblies were used.

Skateboard trucks consist of a base plate (for mounting the truck to the deck), and an axle (located inside the aluminum hanger), which pivots on 3 urethane bushings, called the kingpin bushings and the pivot bushing.

The stiffer the kingpin bushing is, the more stable the ride. This axle system allows for independent suspension and steering of the board. Steering is achieved by leaning left or right.

This picture shows a typical aluminum skateboard hanger (sometimes spelled hangar). The steel axle is located inside the hanger.

When a skater performs a grind, the hanger comes into contact with a grinding surface (metal, coping, plastic, concrete, wood) and begins to slide.

This puts a lot of stress on the truck, and will eventually cause it to fatigue.
It's always a good idea to take an extra hanger, kingpin, hardware, axle nuts, bushings and skate tool with you when you go to the skatepark. You never know when one of these components will break, or fall off or need adjusting.

What are stress cracks?

Stress cracks occur naturally in the wood. The stress cracks become visible when the plys of maple are put into the molds and pressed,. Stress cracks occur in all layers, but are only visible in the outside layers.

Stress cracks normally occur on the nose or tail, and not at the contact points which endure the greatest impact forces. Therefore, most small stress cracks have no effect on overall performance.

What do I do if My Deck Chips or Cracks?

Go to the local hardware store and get some good wood glue. Then, just pour some glue on the broken wood chip and put it back into position on your deck. Use a clamp to hold it in place while it dries.

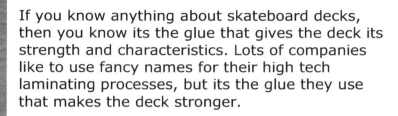

If you know anything about skateboard decks, then you know its the glue that gives the deck its strength and characteristics. Lots of companies like to use fancy names for their high tech laminating processes, but its the glue they use that makes the deck stronger.

If a deck chips a lot or delaminates, then it probably was laminated with cheap glue. If you have some large stress cracks in your deck, fill them in with wood glue. This can extend the life of your deck.

Note: if one of the layers in a deck cracks, then glue won't help. If that happens, it's time for a new deck!

102] 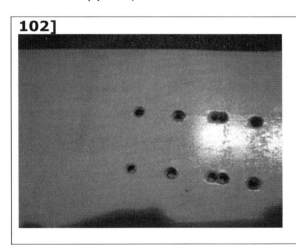	Notice the small stress cracks. I experimented a lot with different wheelbases on this deck. That's why it has so many holes and looks stupid. Anyway, the stress cracks will be bigger than this if you have skated your deck for a while.

To help strengthen this weak area, pour the wood glue over the cracks. . The wood glue should form a bond that is actually stronger than	103]

the wood itself.

104]

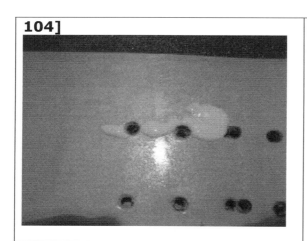

Let the glue seep through the cracks

Wipe off the excess.

105]

Turn the deck over, and repeat.

Summary

To sum it all up, there are some great decks being produced right now and some that are not so great. The biggest key is finding out what is right for you.

It's all about quantity vs. quality.

I get tired of having to grip decks often. I think this is true for most skaters.

We usually get what we can pay for.

Why should skaters care if a deck is made from wood or some type of plastic?

Is it because it is lighter, stronger, more durable, or cheaper? Is it because it is a good starting point for environmentalists to sound out a call for the preservation of our forests?

With the cost of manufacturing and electricity, which is achieved through coal or nuclear energy, and fuel for transportation, not to mention the cost of producing the transportation, the true environmental cost will always be high.

Unfortunately, these restrictions contribute to the movement of factories to developing countries, where laws are flexible at best. And, overseas manufacturers often use inferior woods and glues.

In the end, consumer demand and material availability will be the determining factors.

Printed in Great Britain
by Amazon